Science Mysteries

How Do We Stay on Earth?

A Gravity Mystery

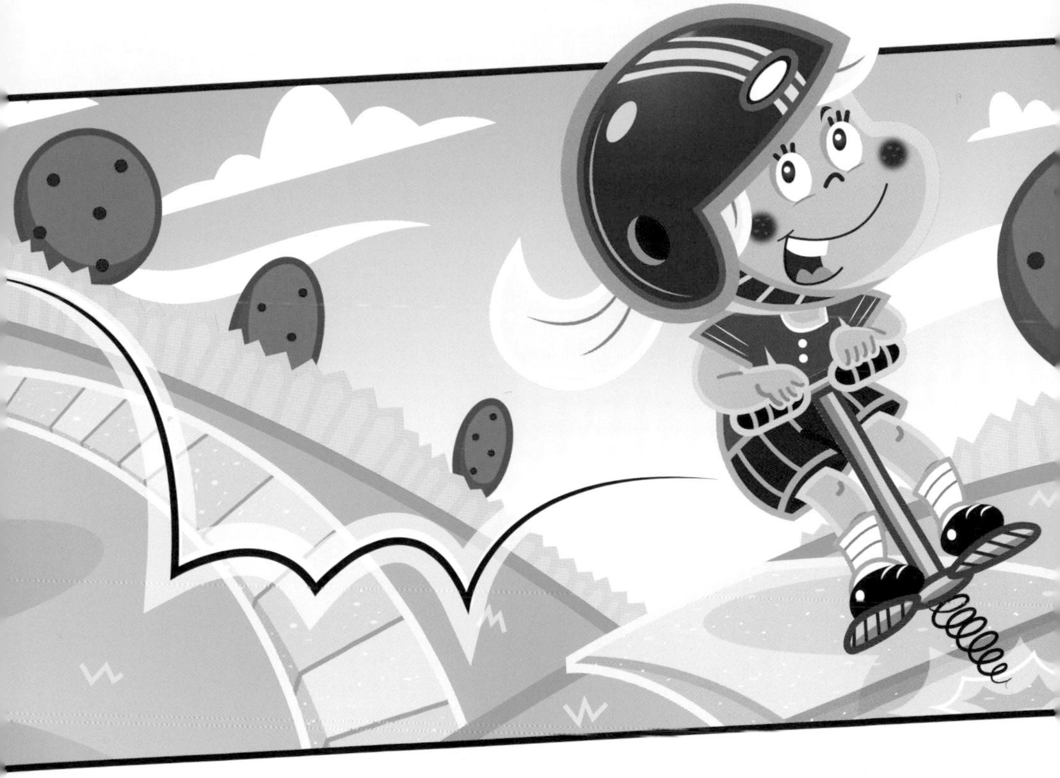

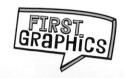

by Amy S. Hansen

illustrated by Korey Scott

Consultant:
Thomas R. Brown, PhD
Assistant Professor of Physics
Minnesota State University, Mankato

First Graphics

Capstone Press
a capstone imprint

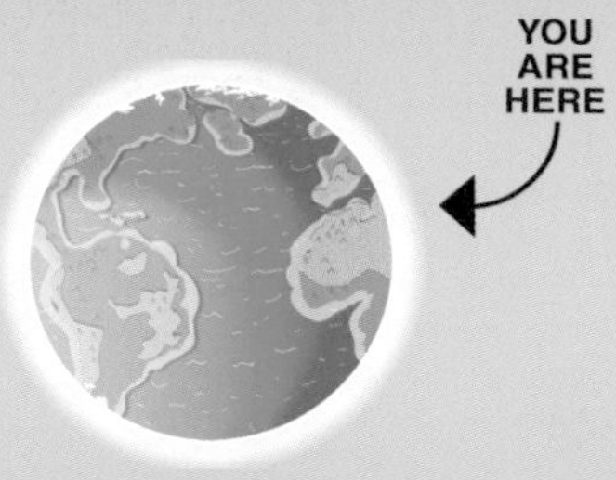
YOU
ARE
HERE

First Graphics are published by Capstone Press,
1710 Roe Crest Drive, North Mankato, Minnesota 56003.
www.capstonepub.com

Library of Congress Cataloging-in-Publication Data
Hansen, Amy.
How do we stay on Earth? : a gravity mystery / by Amy S. Hansen ; illustrated by Korey Scott.
p. cm.—(First graphics. Science mysteries)
Summary: "In graphic novel format, text and illustrations explains the force of gravity and how it keeps us on Earth"—Provided by publisher.
Includes bibliographical references and index.
ISBN 978-1-4296-6097-6 (library binding)
ISBN 978-1-4296-7174-3 (paperback)
1. Gravity—Comic books, strips, etc.—Juvenile literature. 2. Gravitation—Comic books, strips, etc.—Juvenile literature. 3. Graphic novels. I. Scott, Korey, ill. II. Title. III. Series.
QC178.H24 2012
531'.14—dc22 2011001015

EDITOR: CHRISTOPHER L. HARBO
DESIGNER: LORI BYE
ART DIRECTOR: NATHAN GASSMAN
PRODUCTION SPECIALIST: ERIC MANSKE

Printed in the United States 4085

TABLE OF CONTENTS

WHY AM I STUCK ON THE GROUND?

The ground is never far from your feet.

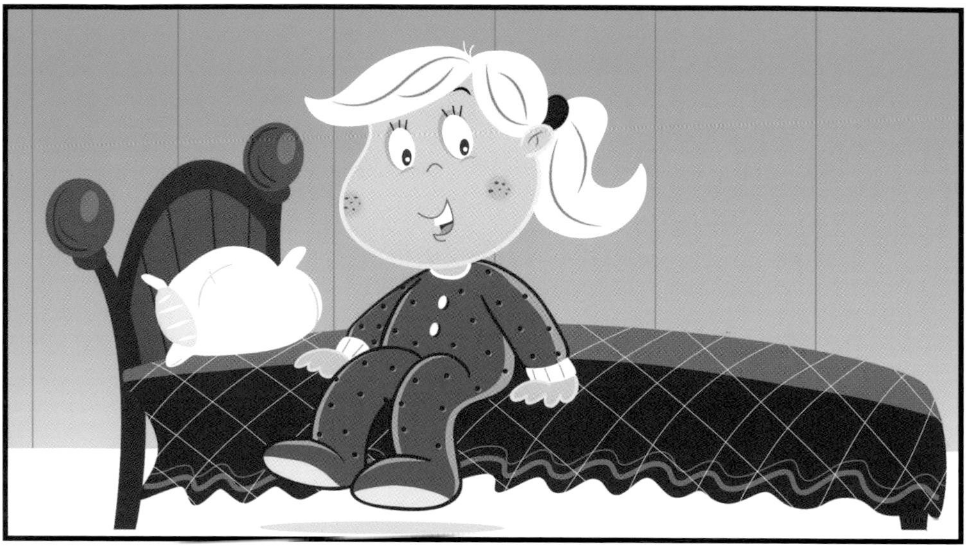

When you get out of bed, your feet hit the floor.

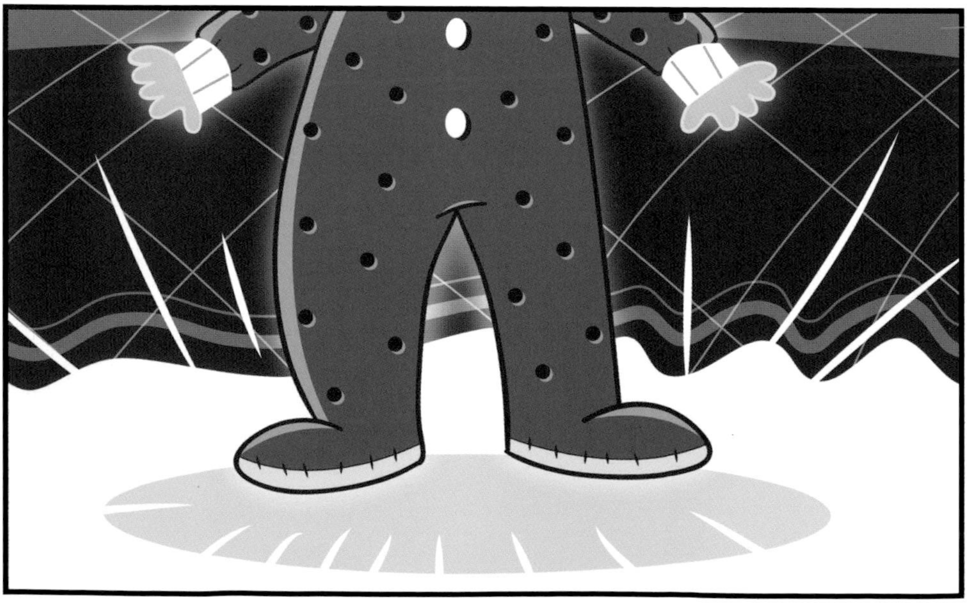

When you run, your feet always return to the ground.

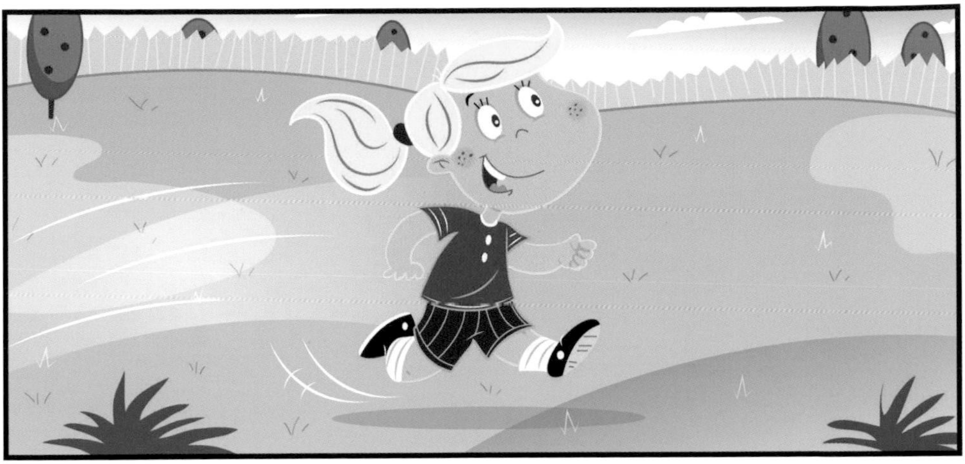

Even when you jump, a force you can't see pulls you back to Earth.

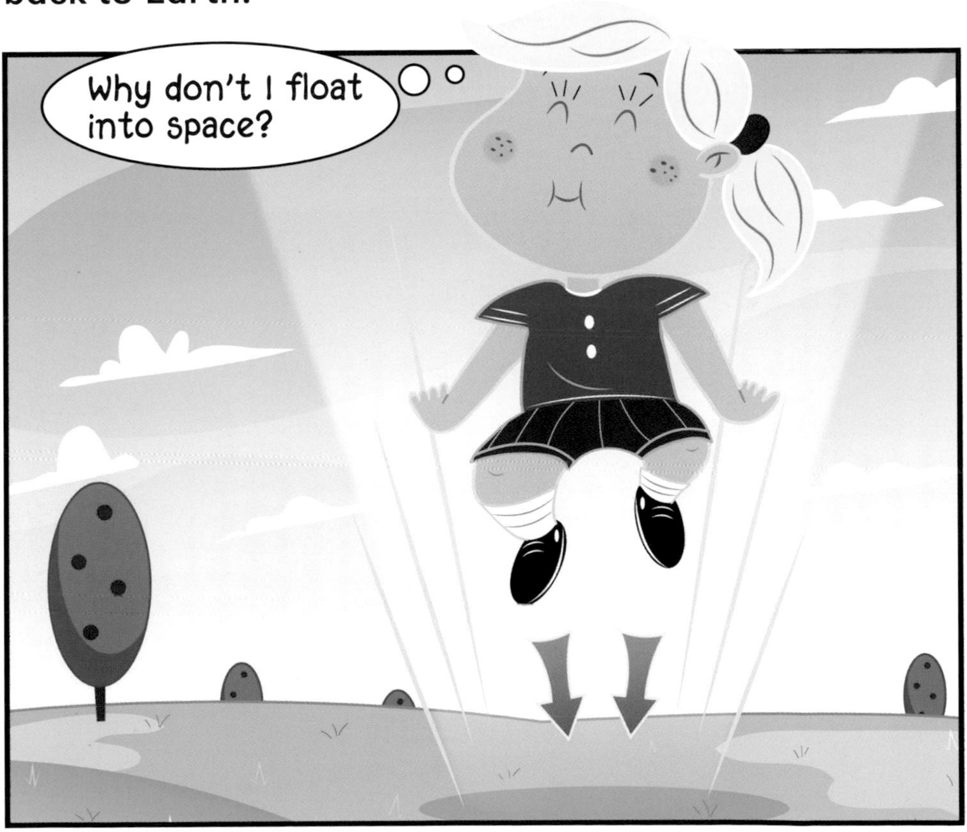
Why don't I float into space?

Gravity is the force that holds you on Earth.

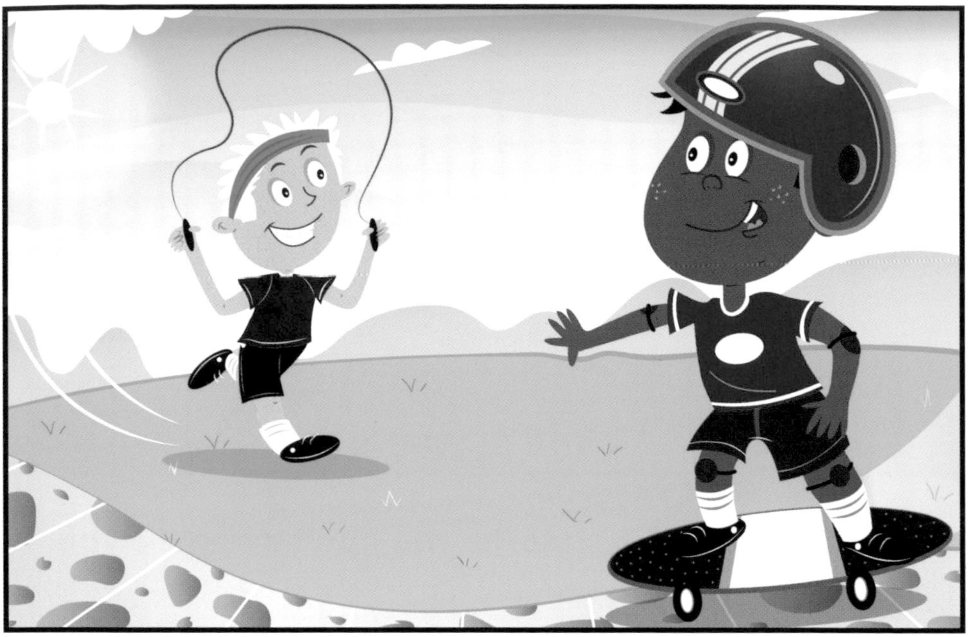

Gravity pulls everything toward the center of the planet.

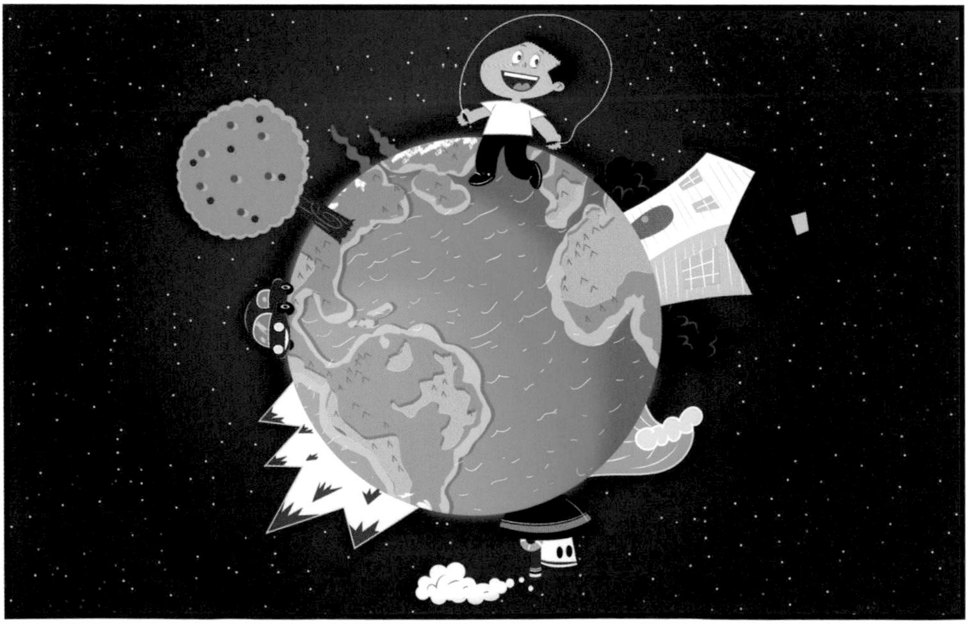

You can't see gravity, but you can see it at work. When you drop an apple, gravity pulls it to the ground.

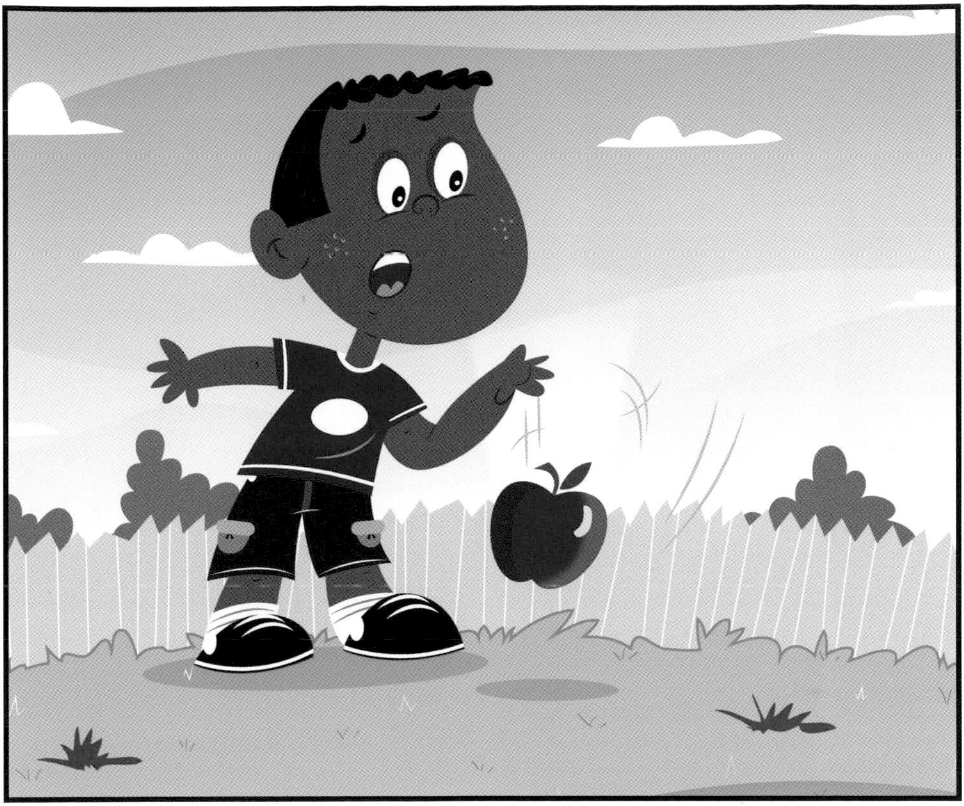

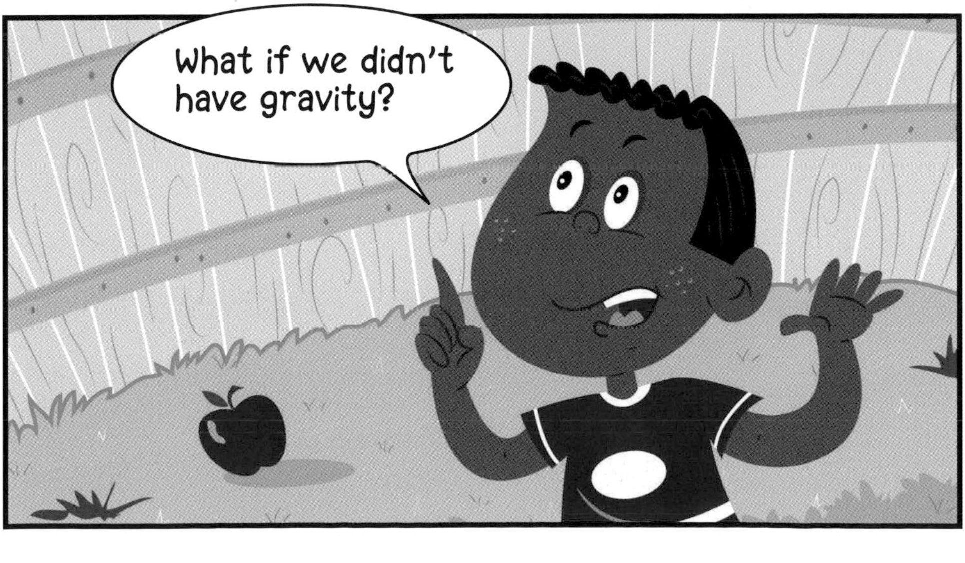
What if we didn't have gravity?

Without gravity, there wouldn't be up or down.

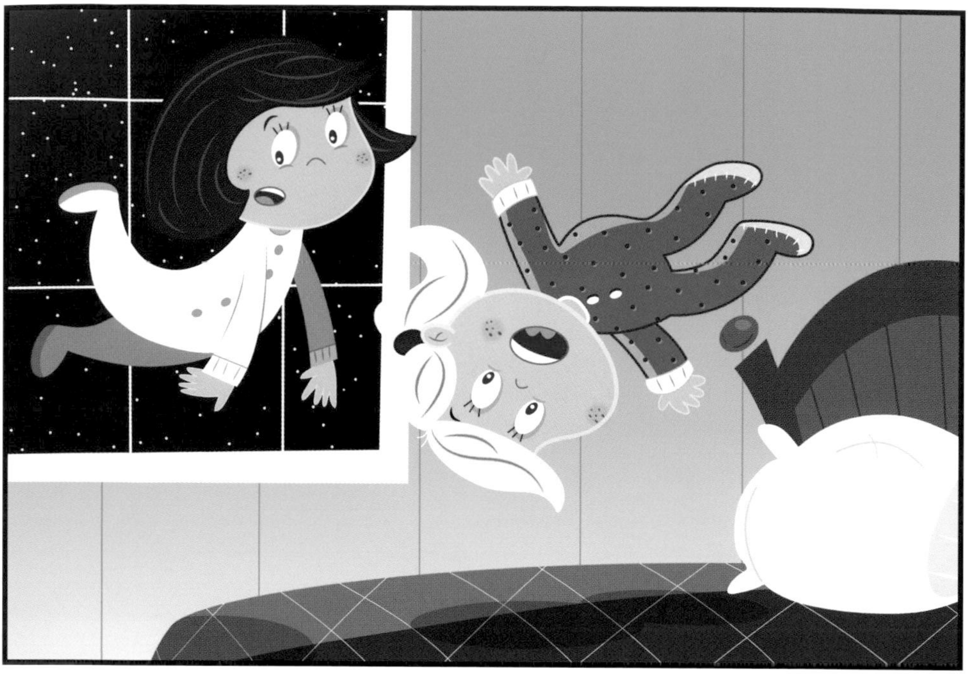

You couldn't lie down, jump up, or sit still to eat.

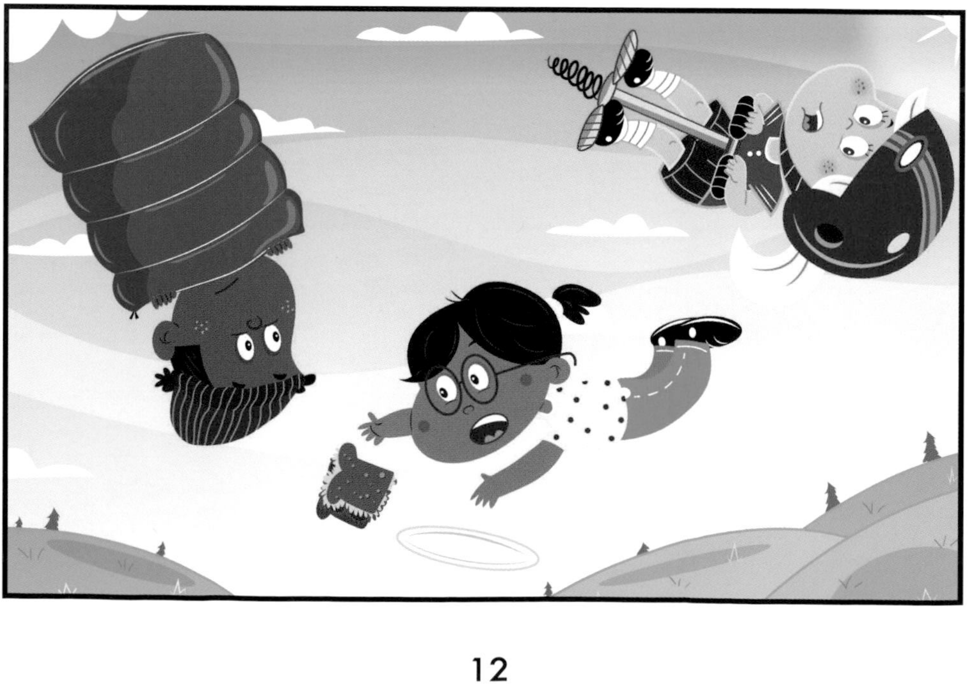

Gravity pulls everything toward the ground.

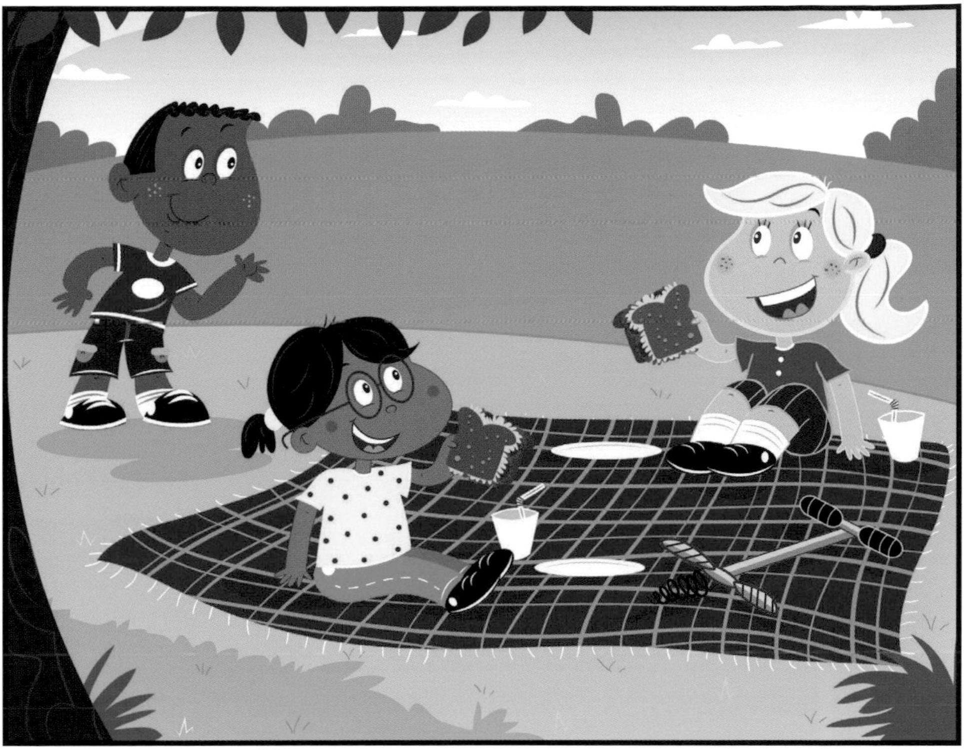

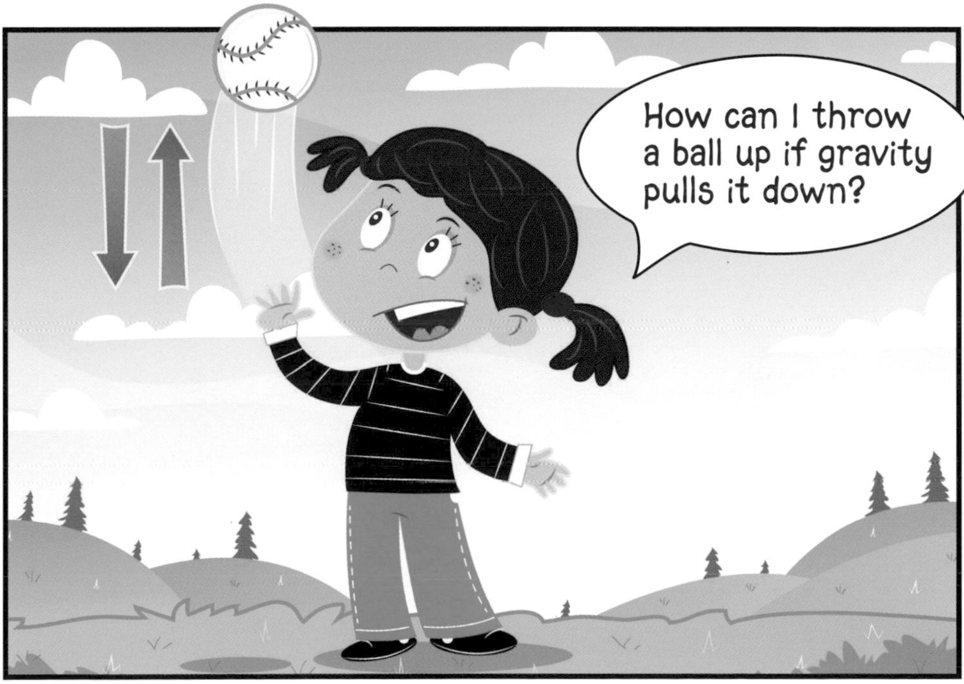
How can I throw a ball up if gravity pulls it down?

Gravity doesn't stop you from throwing a ball. It just keeps you from throwing it very high.

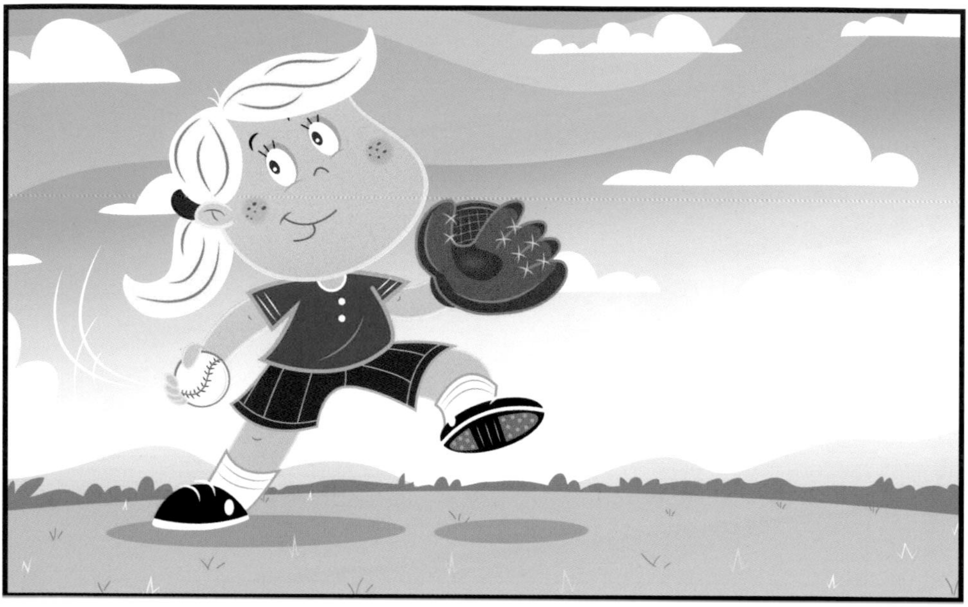

You use a force to throw a ball.

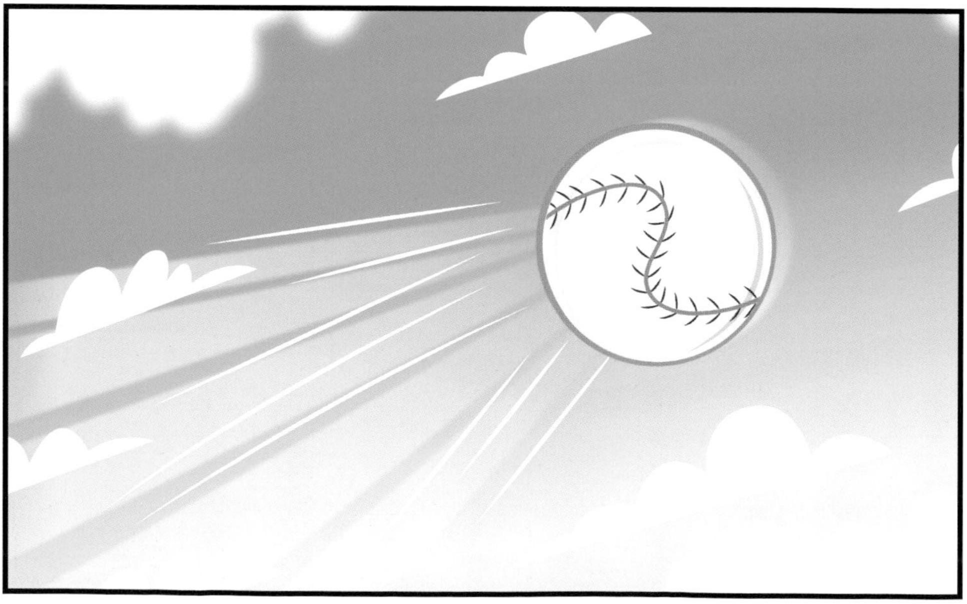

Gravity starts slowing the ball when it leaves your hand.

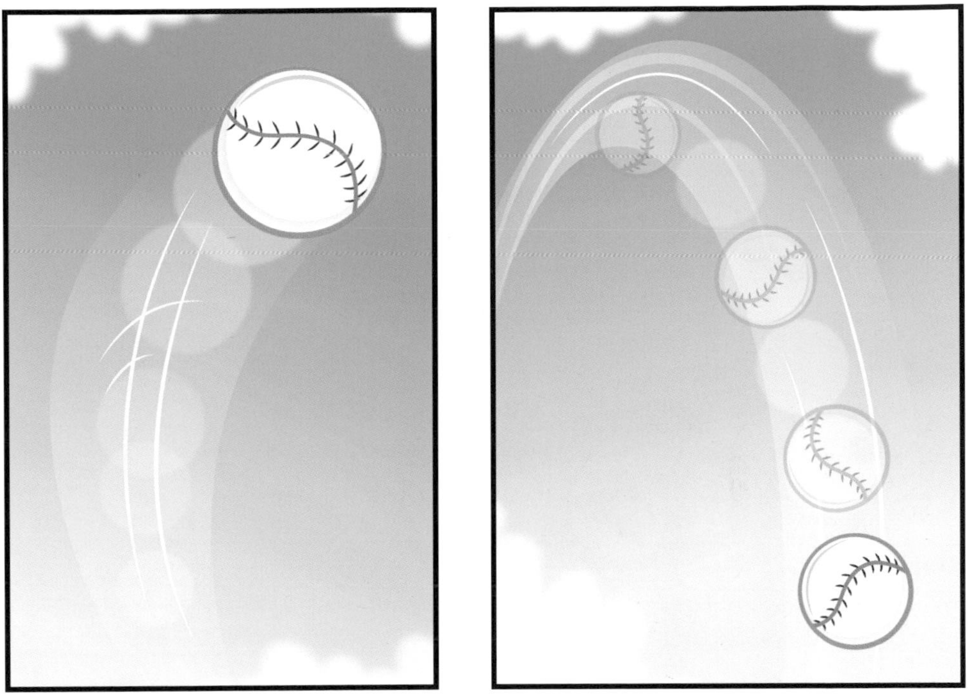

Soon the ball slows to a stop. Gravity pulls it back to Earth.

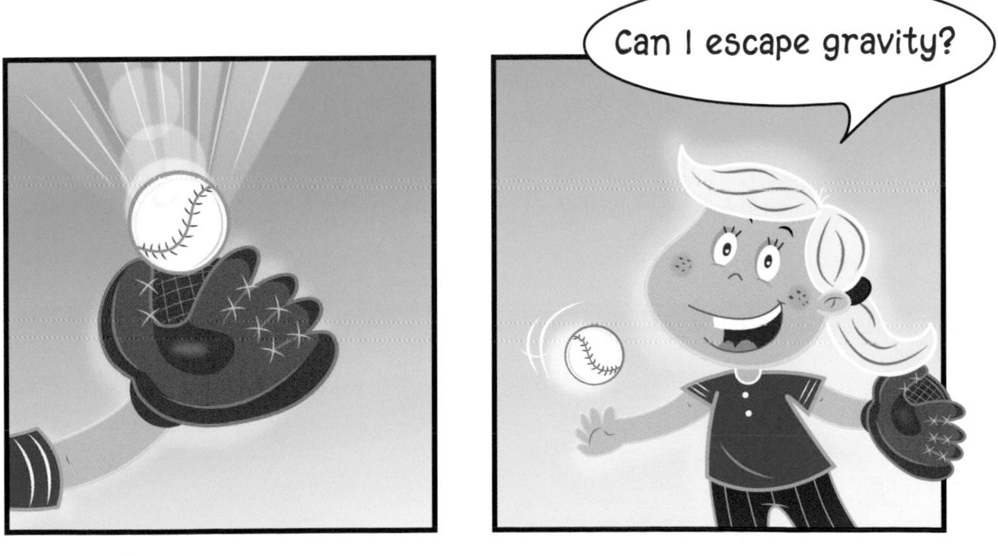
Can I escape gravity?

Where Does Gravity Feel Different?

You can't escape gravity. But gravity can make you feel like you are floating on a roller coaster.

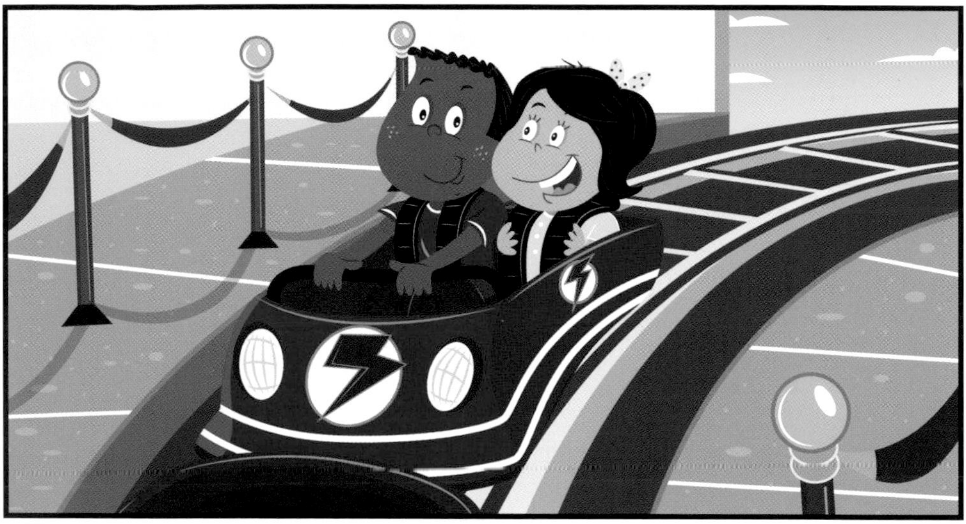

Gravity's pull feels strong when you ride up hill. Your back is pressed into the seat.

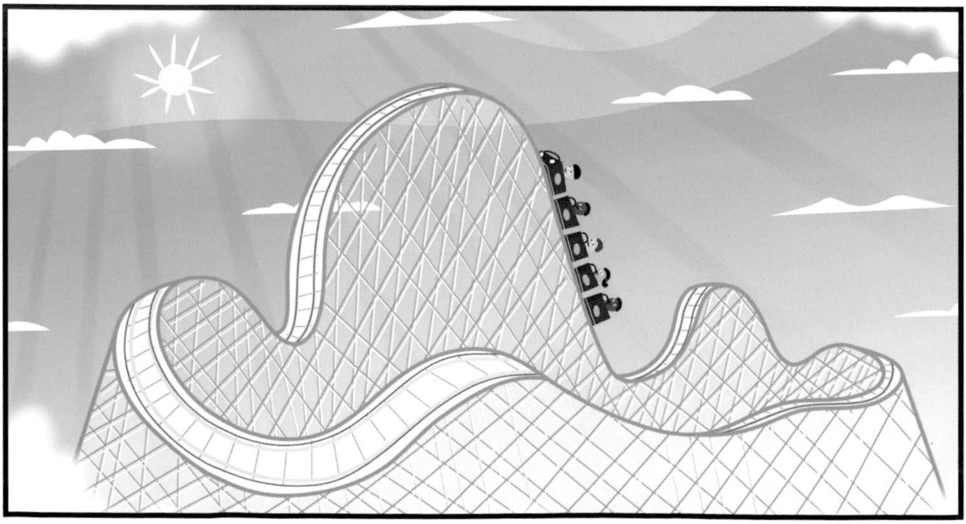

When you reach the top, the ride lets you fall.

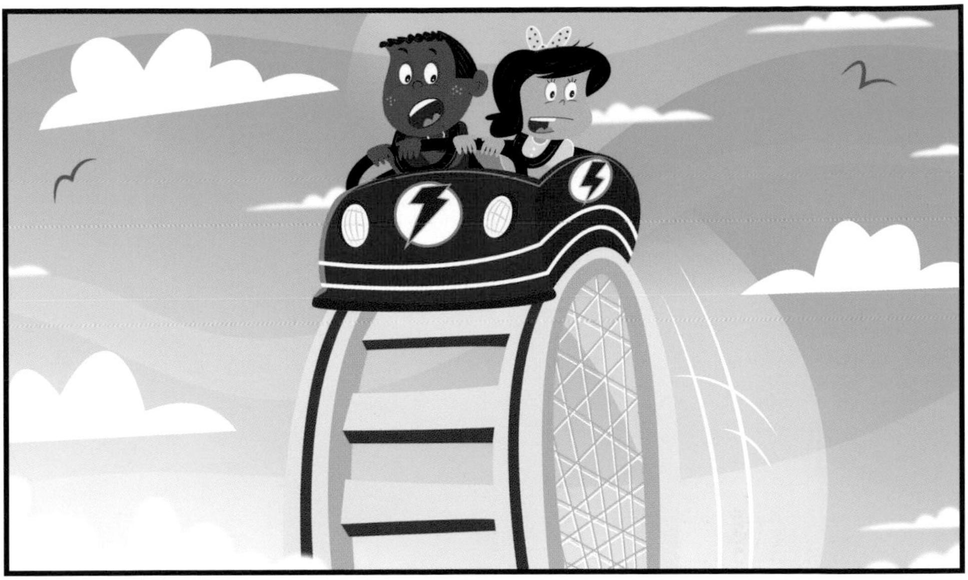

For a moment, your seat doesn't press on you.
You feel like you are floating.

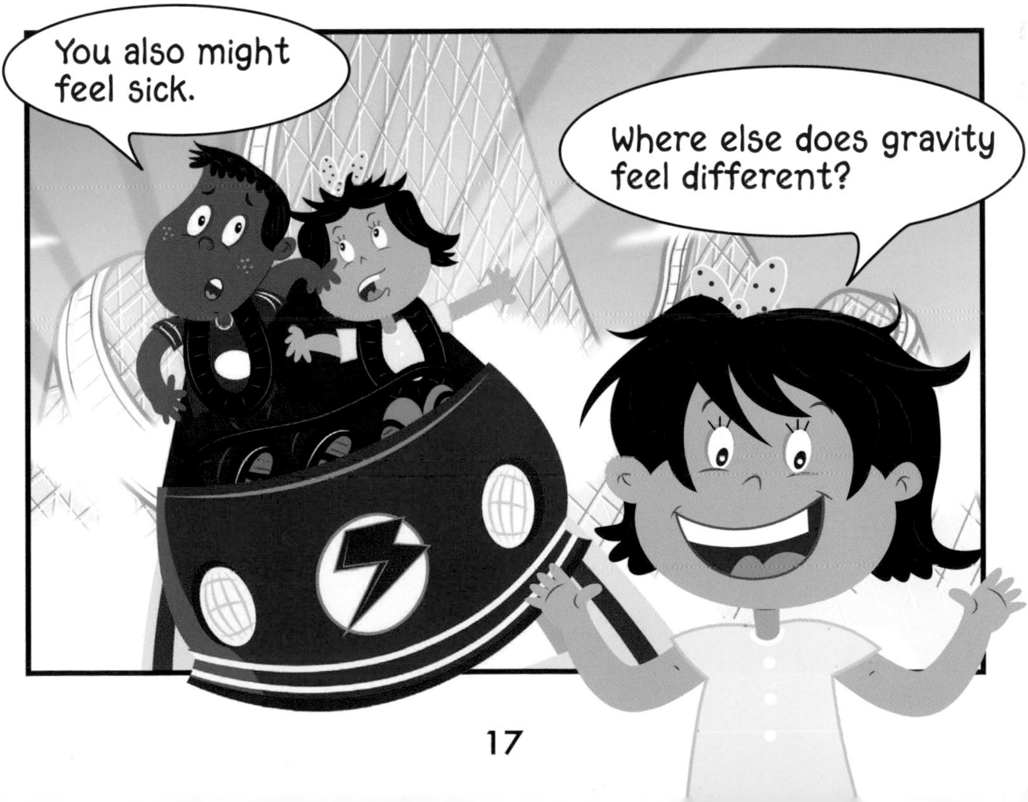
You also might feel sick.
Where else does gravity feel different?

Gravity feels very different on the moon.

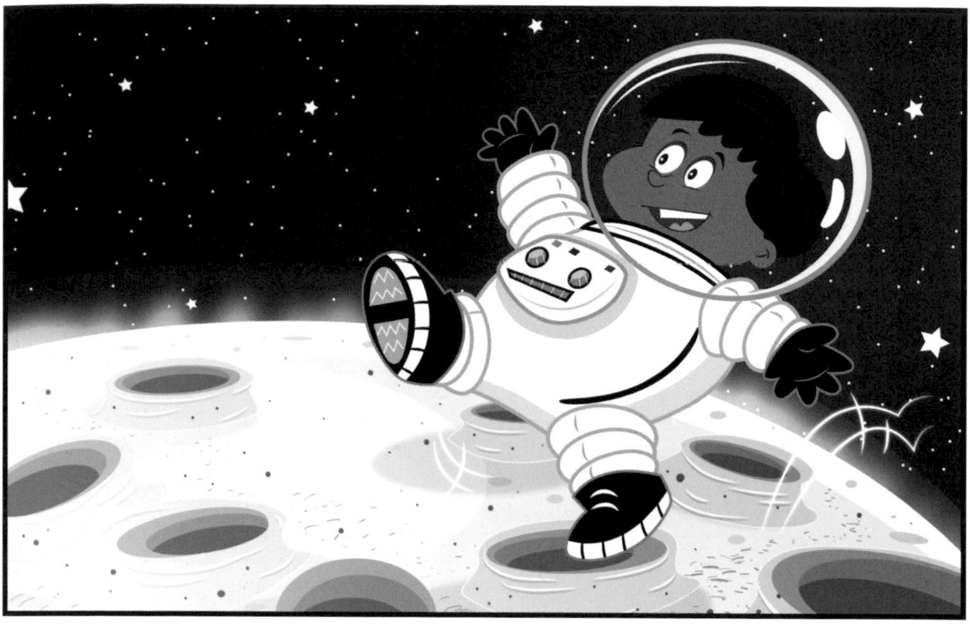

The moon has a smaller mass than Earth. Mass is the amount of matter that makes up an object.

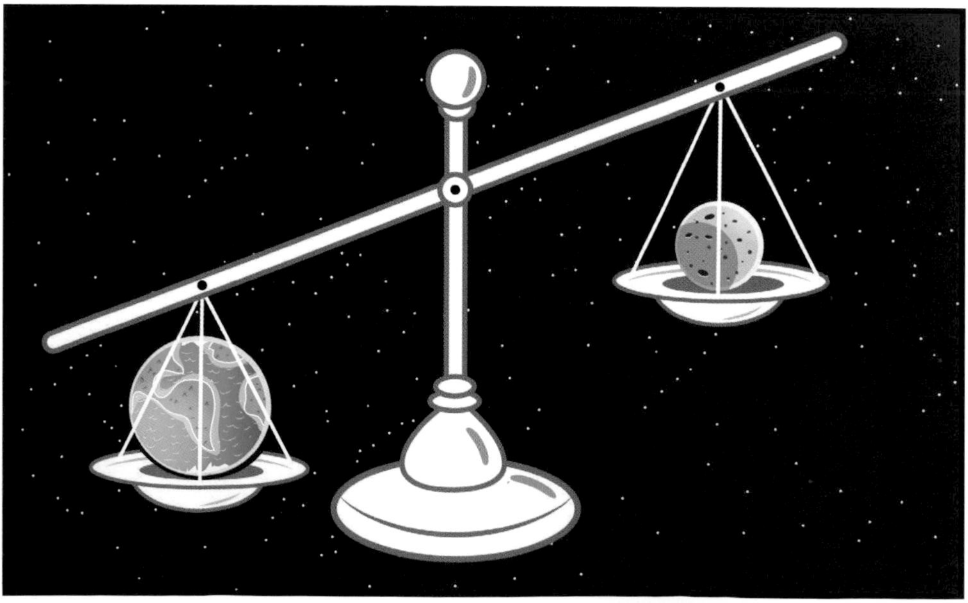

The moon's smaller mass means it has less gravity.

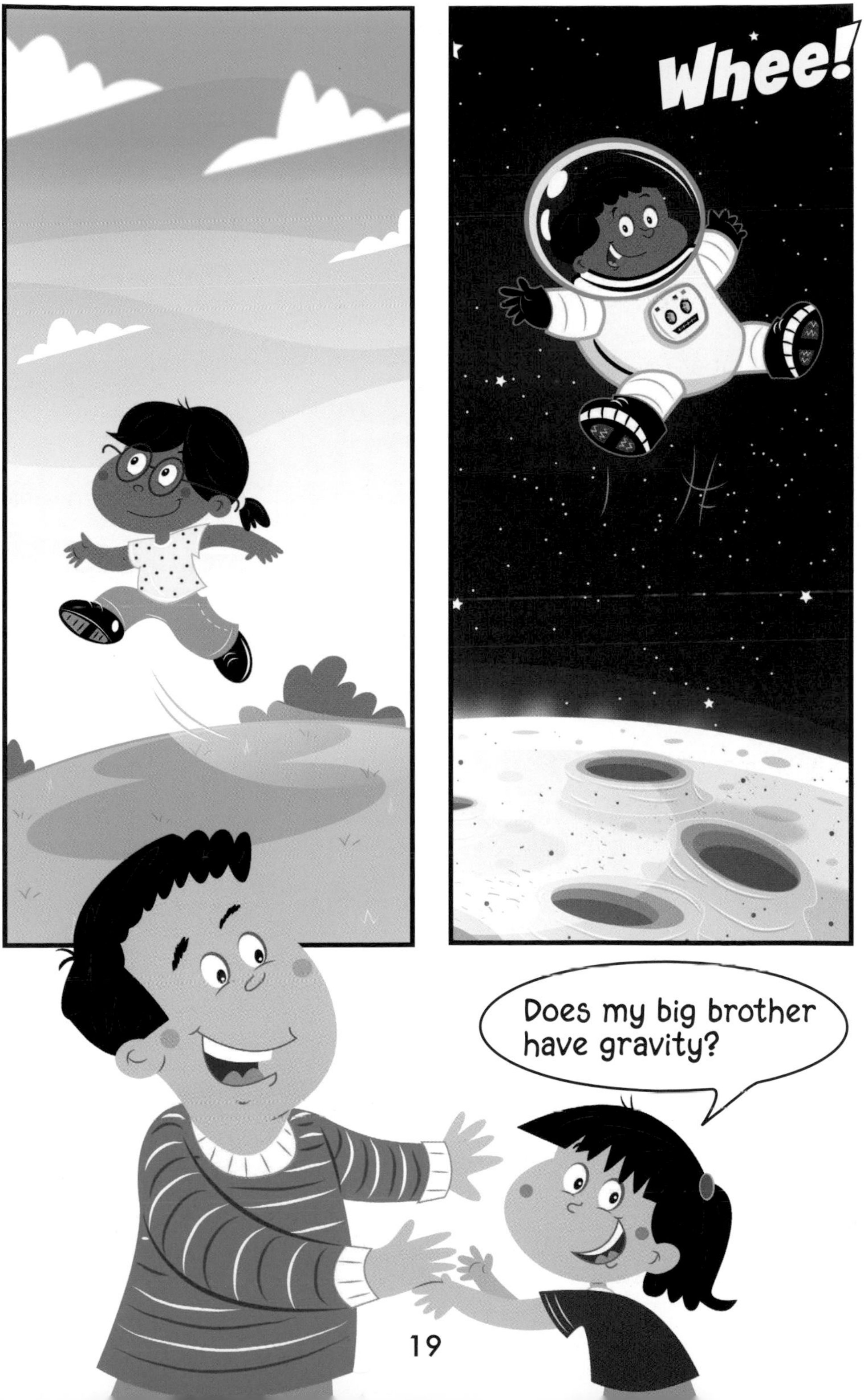
Whee!
Does my big brother have gravity?

Do All Objects Have Gravity?

All objects have some gravity.

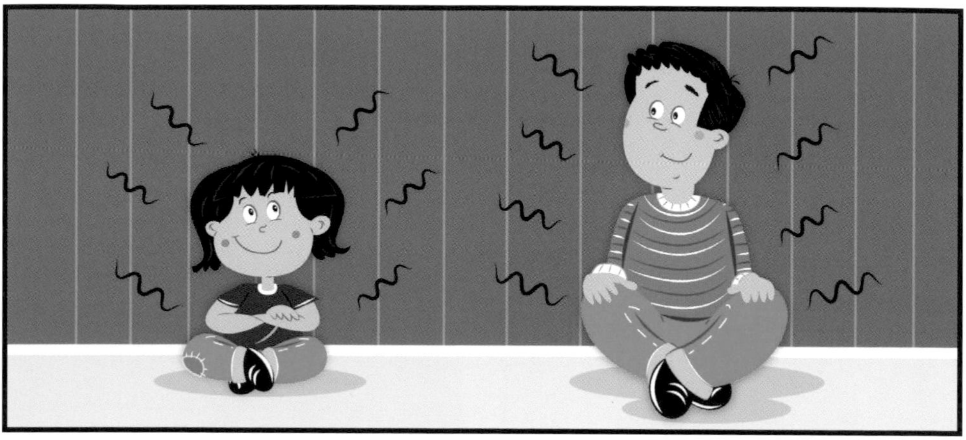

Gravity makes all objects in space pull on each other.

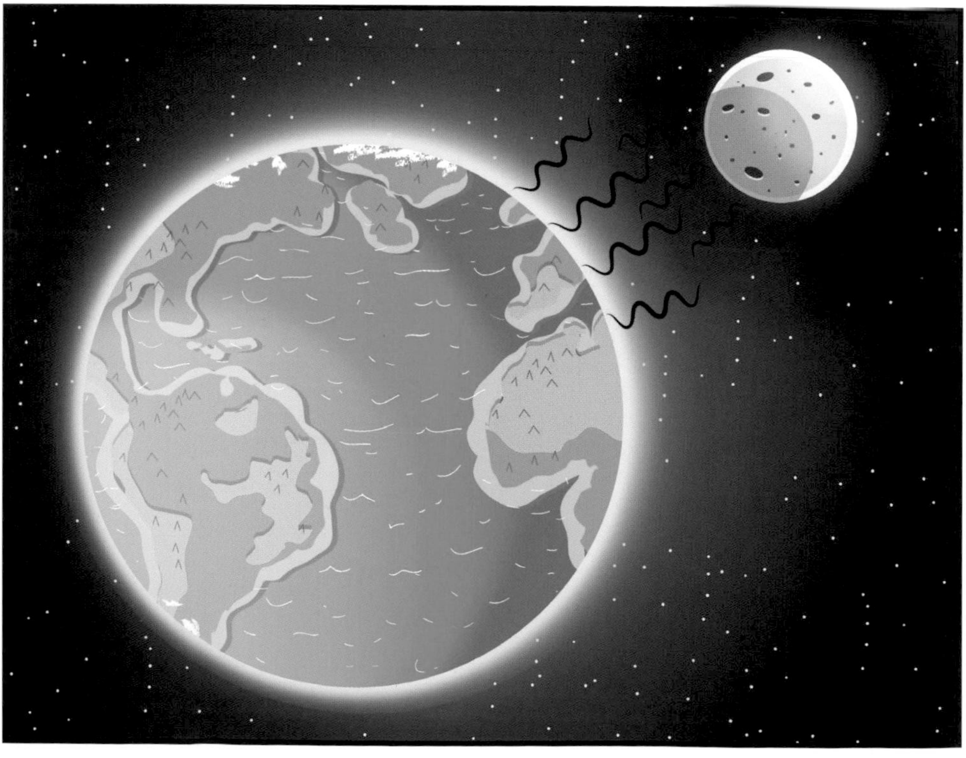

But even the biggest brother is tiny compared to Earth.

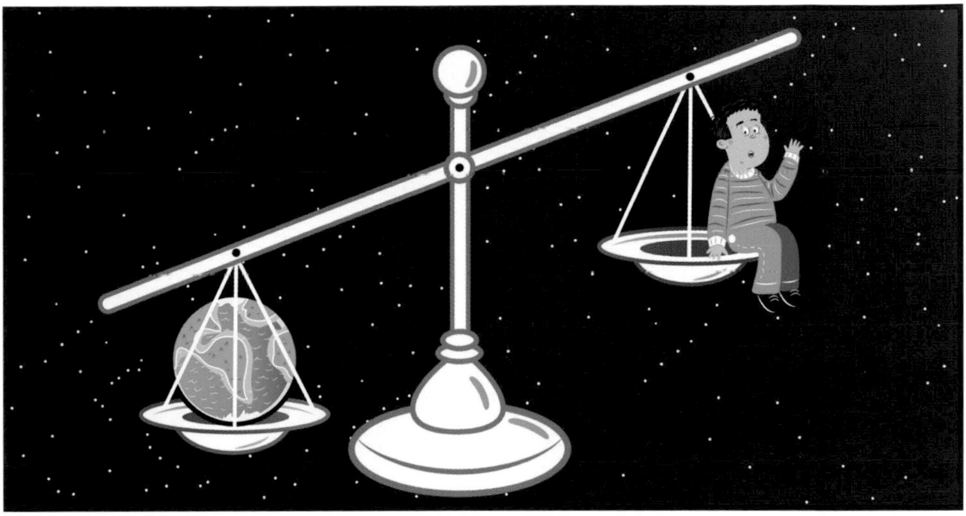

His gravity is too weak for you to feel.

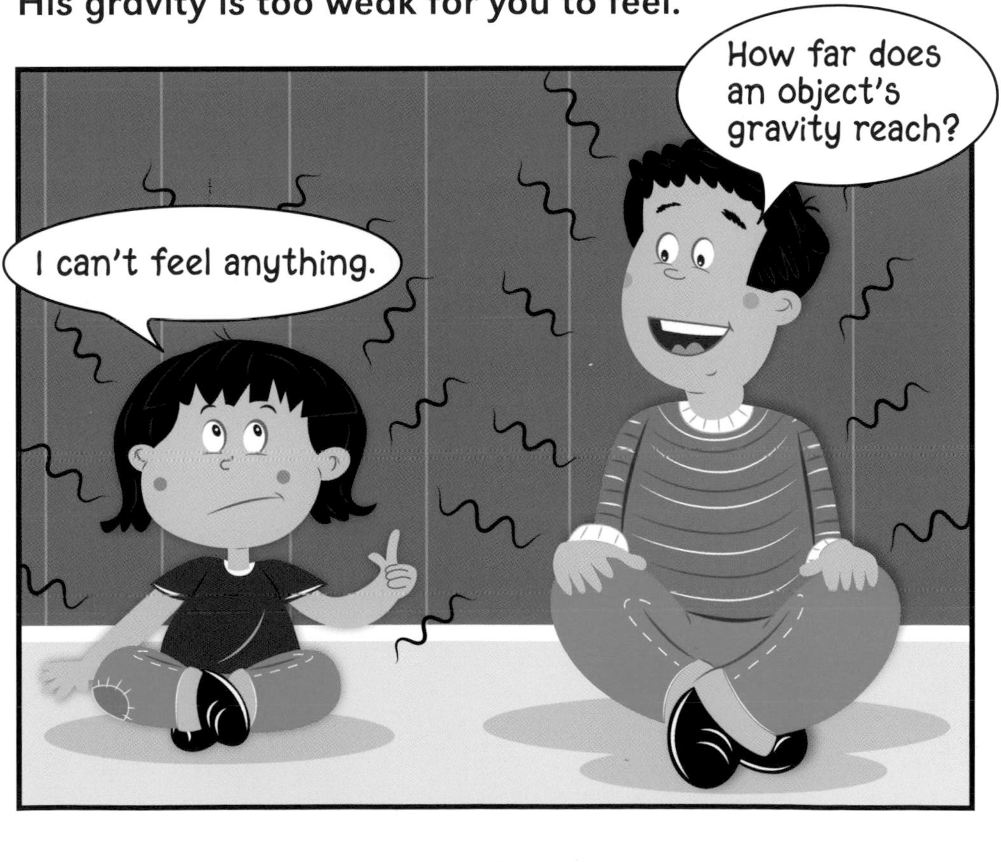
How far does an object's gravity reach?
I can't feel anything.

The more mass an object has, the farther its gravity reaches. Earth's gravity pulls on objects far into space.

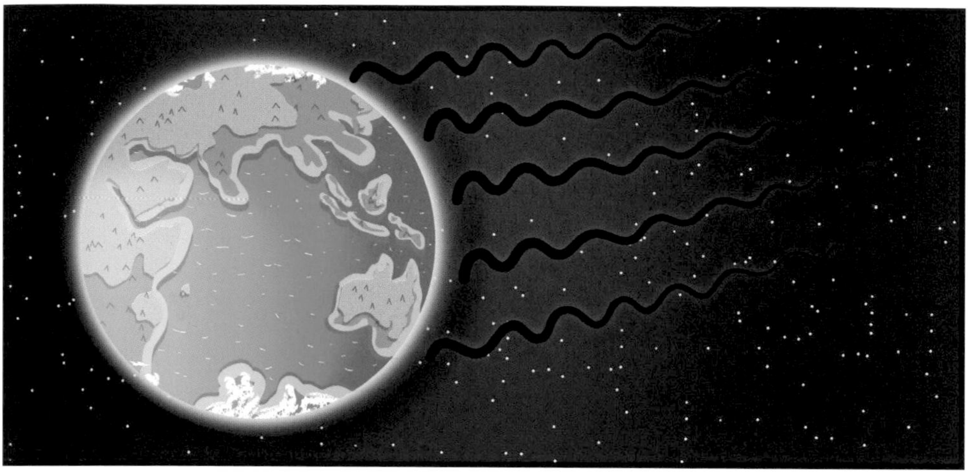

It is strong enough to pull on the moon.

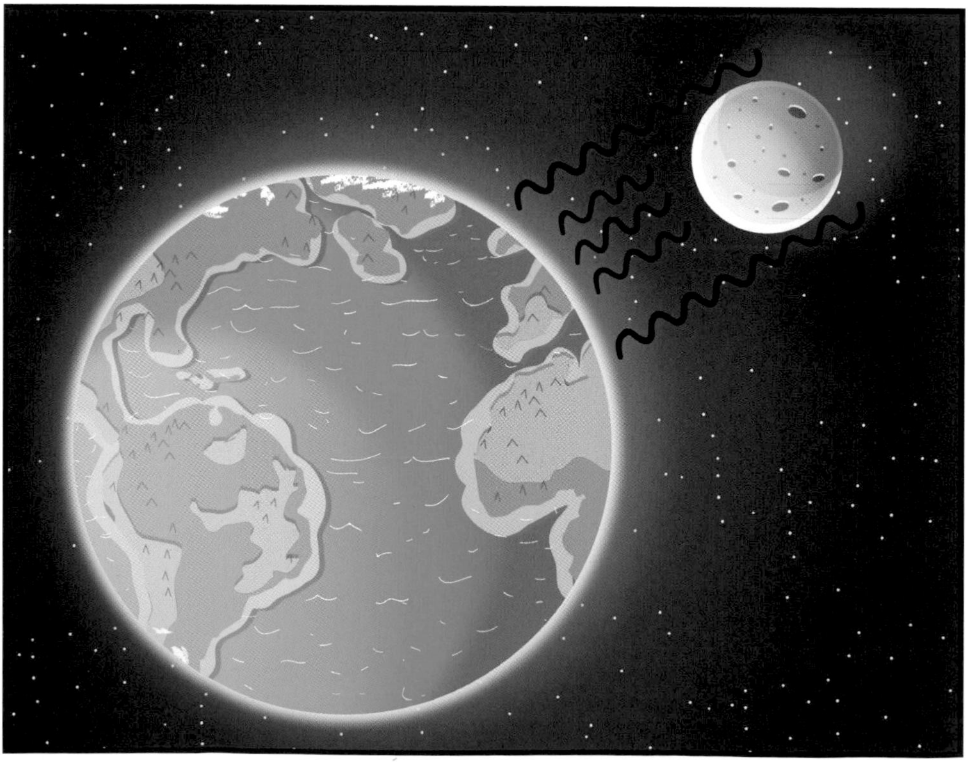

Gravity keeps the moon on its path around Earth.

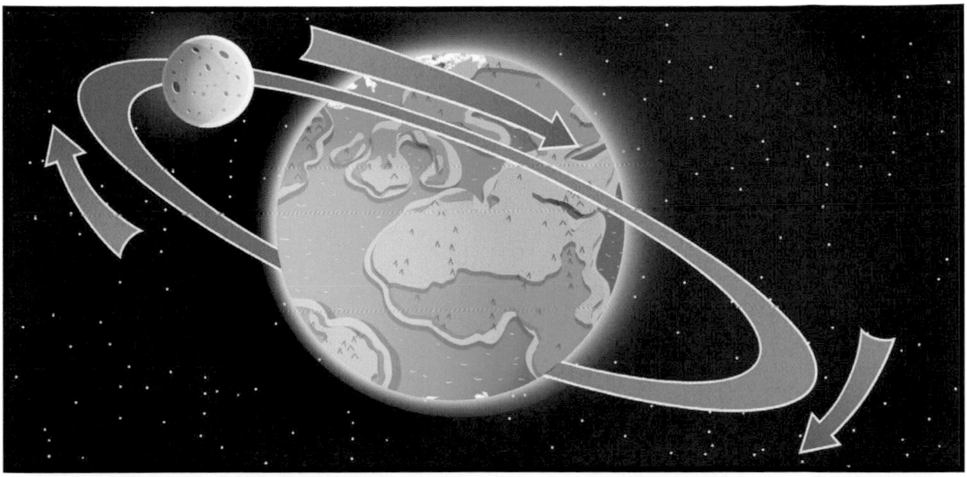

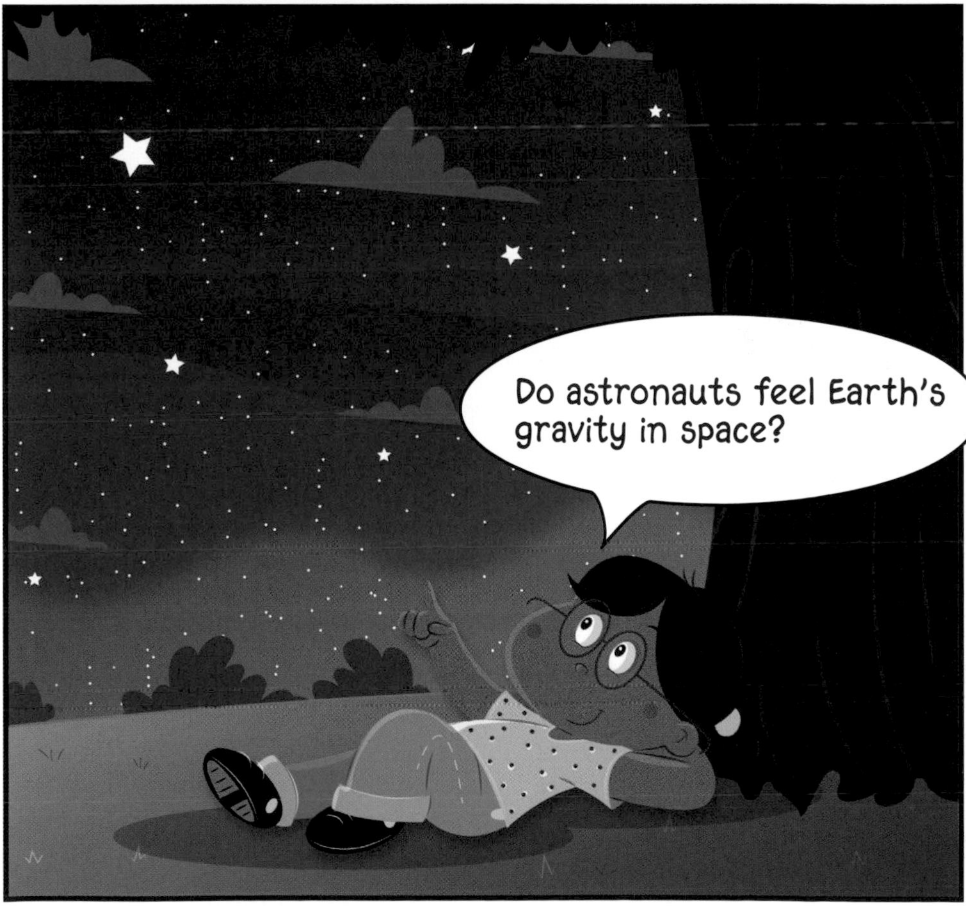
Do astronauts feel Earth's gravity in space?

Earth's gravity pulls on astronauts in space.
They just don't feel it.

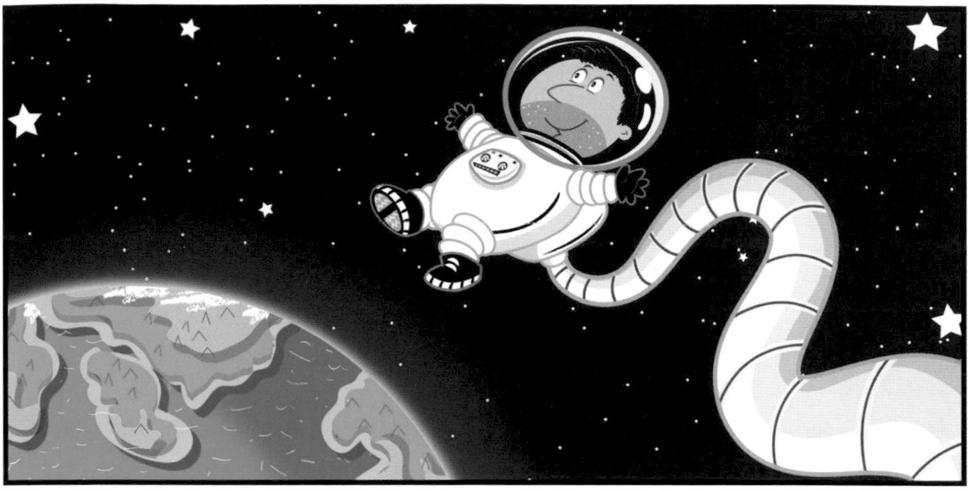

Gravity makes astronauts fall toward Earth.
Earth's curve keeps them from reaching the ground.

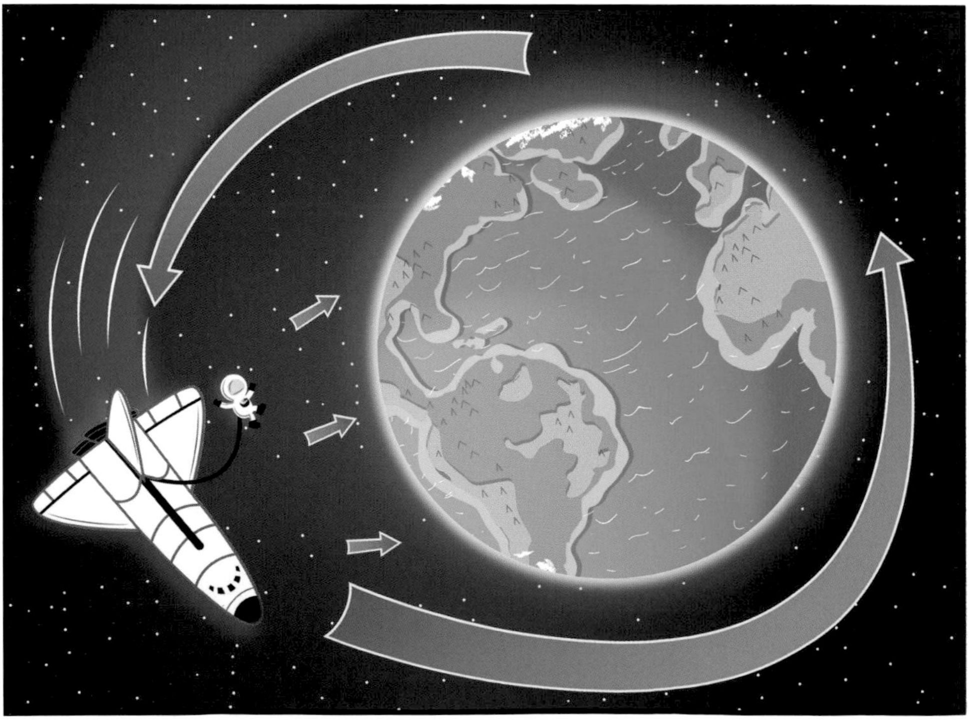

This constant falling motion makes them feel weightless. Being weightless makes life difficult in space.

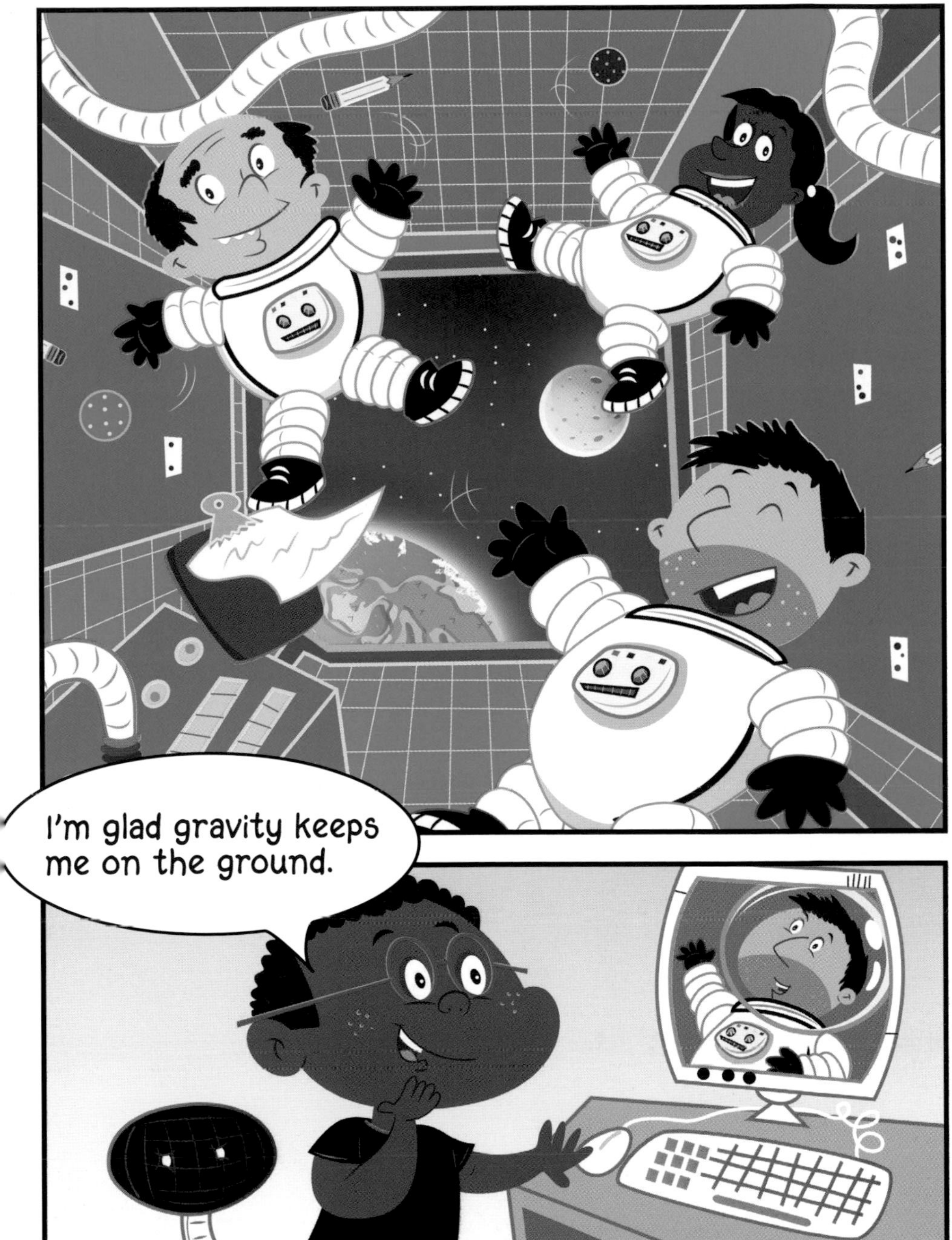
I'm glad gravity keeps
me on the ground.

GLOSSARY

astronaut—a person who travels into space

force—a push or a pull on an object

gravity—the force that pulls objects toward the center of Earth

mass—the amount of matter in an object

matter—anything that has weight and takes up space

weightless—free of the feeling of gravity

READ MORE

Boothroyd, Jennifer. *What Holds Us to Earth?: A Look at Gravity.* First Physics. Minneapolis: Lerner Publications Co., 2011.

Monroe, Tilda. *What Do You Know about Forces and Motion?* 20 Questions. New York: PowerKids Press, 2011.

Moore, Rob. *Why Do Balls Bounce?: All about Gravity.* Solving Science Mysteries. New York: PowerKids Press, 2010.

INTERNET SITES

FactHound offers a safe, fun way to find Internet sites related to this book. All of the sites on FactHound have been researched by our staff.

Here's all you do:

Visit *www.facthound.com*

Type in this code: 9781429660976

 **Super-cool stuff!** Check out projects, games and lots more at **www.capstonekids.com**

INDEX

SCIENCE MYSTERIES

TITLES IN THIS SET:

HOW DO WE KNOW ABOUT DINOSAURS?
A FOSSIL MYSTERY

HOW DO WE STAY ON EARTH?
A GRAVITY MYSTERY

WHERE DO THE BIRDS GO?
A MIGRATION MYSTERY

WHERE DOES THE SUN GO AT NIGHT?
AN EARTH SCIENCE MYSTERY